Marketing Your Local History Museum

Compiled by

Alfred Brock

The Local Historical Museum

Contents

A history museum can provide several benefits to a small city. Here are some key advantages: 6

Why is Cultural Preservation important to a small American city? 7

Why is Education and Learning about local history important to a small American city? 10

Why is Tourism and Economic Impact related to local history important to a small American city? 12

Why is Community Engagement spurred by the history of the place important to a small American city? 15

Why is Research and Scholarship related to social, natural, business and scientific history of an area important to a small American city? 18

How can the Quality of Life in a community be enhanced through the presentation of local historical information be important to a small American city? 21

How can local history be used to promote Civic Engagement in a small American city? 24

Farmington Community Library Grants Collection 27

Potential Partnerships or Projects 29

Working with the Collection 32

Raising Visibility 35

Volunteerism 41

Non-Profit and Corporate Support 46

Alternatives for the Future 51

    Immediate Actions 51

    Patents 53

Here are 30 fundraising ideas for a small city history museum: 56

Here are the names of 100 organizations that provide grants to small history museums. Please note that grant availability may vary, and it's important to research each organization for specific eligibility criteria and application details: 59

Fundraising can be fun and interesting – 64

Cooperation among departments in an organization is crucial for several reasons: 68

Opportunities for Research and Invention 73

Methods of Communication to Increase Cooperation 77

On the Matter of Products that can be offered by the Museum from presently available materials 81

  Here is a list of printed and digital materials created from historical images that can be offered for sale: 81

  Reproductions 83

  Learn how to write grants and solicit funds : 86

  Support Materials to Gain Public Attention and Prepare for Fundraising 87

A history museum can provide several benefits to a small city. Here are some key advantages:

Cultural Preservation: A history museum serves as a repository of a city's historical artifacts, documents, and stories. It helps preserve the cultural heritage and collective memory of the community. By showcasing local history, the museum ensures that the city's traditions, customs, and achievements are not forgotten.

Education and Learning: Museums offer valuable educational opportunities. They provide a platform for residents, particularly students, to learn about the history of their city, region, or country. Exhibits, interactive displays, and educational programs help visitors gain a deeper understanding of the past, fostering a sense of appreciation and curiosity.

Tourism and Economic Impact: A well-curated history museum can attract tourists from both near and far. Visitors interested in the city's history and culture are more likely to stay longer, spend money at local businesses, and support the tourism industry. This influx of tourists can boost the local economy and create new job opportunities.

Community Engagement: History museums often become community hubs, hosting events, lectures, workshops, and exhibitions that engage residents. These activities promote a sense of community pride and identity, encouraging residents to actively participate in their city's history and cultural heritage. Museums also provide meeting spaces for local organizations and can serve as venues for community celebrations.

Research and Scholarship: History museums contribute to academic research and scholarship. They often collaborate with historians, archaeologists, and other experts to conduct research, curate exhibits, and publish works. These collaborations enhance the city's scholarly reputation and may attract scholars and researchers to the area.

Enhancing Quality of Life: A history museum adds to the overall quality of life in a small city. It offers a unique and enriching experience for residents, providing opportunities for leisure, reflection, and intellectual stimulation. Museums often organize special exhibitions or events that cater to diverse interests, making them accessible and enjoyable for people of all ages.

Promoting Civic Engagement: History museums can inspire civic engagement by showcasing stories of activism, social change, and community development. By highlighting past struggles and achievements, they encourage citizens to actively participate in shaping the future of their city. Museums may also host discussions and programs on relevant contemporary issues, fostering dialogue and encouraging civic participation.

In summary, history museums provide numerous benefits to a small city, including cultural preservation, education, economic impact, community engagement, research opportunities, enhanced quality of life, and promotion of civic engagement. They play a vital role in connecting residents with their past, promoting a sense of pride and identity, and contributing to the overall well-being of the community.

Why is Cultural Preservation important to a small American city?

Cultural preservation is important to a small American city for several reasons:

Identity and Heritage: Cultural preservation helps small cities maintain a sense of identity and pride in their unique history and traditions. It ensures that future generations can understand and appreciate the cultural heritage that defines their community. By preserving local customs, languages, art forms, and historical landmarks, a city can retain its distinct character and foster a strong community bond.

Sense of Belonging: Cultural preservation provides a sense of belonging for residents. When a small city actively preserves its cultural heritage, it creates a shared narrative and common ground for its inhabitants. This shared heritage can strengthen social cohesion, build community connections, and promote a sense of place, where residents feel rooted and connected to their surroundings.

Tourism and Economic Development: Cultural preservation can have positive economic impacts. A small city that safeguards its cultural heritage becomes an attractive destination for tourists seeking authentic experiences. Visitors interested in history, art, music, traditional crafts, or local festivals are more likely to visit and spend money in such a city. This tourism can stimulate the local economy, create jobs, and support small businesses.

Education and Learning: Cultural preservation provides valuable educational opportunities. It allows residents, particularly young people, to learn about their city's history, values, and traditions. By understanding the past, residents can develop a deeper appreciation for their cultural heritage and gain a sense of continuity with previous generations. Cultural preservation also promotes intergenerational knowledge transfer, ensuring that traditional skills and knowledge are passed down to future generations.

Cultural Diversity and Inclusion: Small American cities often have diverse cultural communities, reflecting the nation's rich multicultural fabric. Cultural preservation allows for the recognition and celebration of this diversity. By valuing and preserving the cultural expressions of different groups within the community, a city promotes inclusivity and respect for all residents, fostering a more tolerant and harmonious society.

Preservation of Historic Sites and Architecture: Cultural preservation often involves the protection of historic sites, buildings, and landmarks. These physical remnants of the past contribute to the unique character of a small city. Preserving them not only maintains the aesthetic appeal but also safeguards important links to the city's history, architecture, and design. Historic preservation can also attract heritage enthusiasts, architects, and scholars interested in studying and appreciating architectural styles and urban development.

In summary, cultural preservation is essential to a small American city as it helps maintain identity, fosters a sense of belonging, supports tourism and economic development, provides educational opportunities, promotes cultural diversity and inclusion, and safeguards historic sites and architecture. By valuing and preserving their cultural heritage, small cities can thrive, attract visitors, and create a strong foundation for the future.

Why is Education and Learning about local history important to a small American city?

Education and learning about local history are important to a small American city for several reasons:

Sense of Identity and Belonging: Learning about local history helps residents develop a sense of identity and belonging to their community. It allows them to understand the unique aspects of their city's past, including significant events, influential figures, and cultural heritage. This knowledge fosters a sense of pride, connection, and loyalty among residents, strengthening the community fabric.

Preservation of Cultural Heritage: Education about local history ensures the preservation of a city's cultural heritage. By learning about the historical traditions, customs, and values of their community, residents can appreciate and pass on these cultural elements to future generations. It helps maintain and celebrate the unique identity and character of the small American city.

Appreciation of Local Landmarks and Architecture: Understanding local history provides insights into the development of a city's landmarks, architecture, and urban planning. Residents can appreciate the significance of historical buildings, neighborhoods, and public spaces that contribute to the city's physical landscape. This knowledge encourages the preservation and maintenance of these architectural treasures.

Community Engagement and Civic Pride: Education about local history promotes community engagement and civic pride. When residents have a deeper understanding of their city's past, they are more likely to actively participate in community activities, local governance, and preservation efforts. It fosters a sense of responsibility towards the city's development and encourages residents to contribute to its growth and well-being.

Connection to National History: Local history is often intertwined with national history. Learning about local events, figures, or movements can provide a broader understanding of how they fit into the larger narrative of American history. It allows residents to connect their own experiences and stories to the broader historical context, fostering a sense of national pride and a deeper appreciation for the country's heritage.

Tourism and Economic Impact: Education and learning about local history can contribute to tourism and economic development. A small American city with a rich historical background can attract visitors interested in exploring the local heritage. Historical sites, museums, and cultural events related to the city's history can become tourist attractions, boosting local businesses and creating job opportunities in the tourism industry.

In summary, education and learning about local history are important to a small American city as they foster a sense of identity and belonging, preserve cultural heritage, promote community engagement and civic pride, enhance appreciation of local landmarks, connect to national history, and contribute to tourism and economic development. By understanding and valuing their own history, residents can actively participate in shaping the future of their community.

Why is Tourism and Economic Impact related to local history important to a small American city?

Tourism and the economic impact related to local history are crucial to a small American city for several reasons:

Economic Growth and Job Creation: Tourism fueled by local history can be a significant driver of economic growth for a small city. Visitors interested in exploring the city's historical sites, landmarks, and cultural heritage contribute to the local economy by spending money on accommodations, dining, shopping, transportation, and entertainment. This influx of tourism can generate revenue for local businesses and create job opportunities in various sectors such as hospitality, retail, and transportation.

Diversification of the Local Economy: Emphasizing local history as a tourism attraction allows a small city to diversify its economic base. Relying on a single industry can make a city vulnerable to economic downturns. However, by leveraging its historical significance, a small city can attract tourists year-round and mitigate the impact of seasonal fluctuations. This diversification strengthens the local economy and enhances its resilience.

Preservation of Historical Sites and Landmarks: Tourism driven by local history often necessitates the preservation and maintenance of historical sites, landmarks, and cultural assets. This focus on preservation ensures the protection and conservation of the city's historical resources for future generations. It encourages investment in restoration, revitalization, and upkeep, leading to the preservation of architectural treasures and contributing to the city's overall aesthetic appeal.

Community Development and Infrastructure Improvement: The economic impact of tourism related to local history can benefit the community by spurring infrastructure development and community improvements. As tourism increases, the demand for amenities and services also grows. This prompts investments in infrastructure projects, such as improved transportation systems, enhanced visitor facilities, and the development of cultural institutions. These developments can not only enhance the visitor experience but also benefit local residents.

Promotion of Local Businesses and Entrepreneurship: Tourism driven by local history provides opportunities for small businesses and entrepreneurs within the community. Local artisans, craftspeople, and entrepreneurs can capitalize on the demand for authentic local products, souvenirs, and experiences. This promotes entrepreneurship, creativity, and innovation, allowing local businesses to thrive and contribute to the economic vitality of the small city.

Enhanced Community Pride and Sense of Identity: Tourism related to local history often brings attention and recognition to a small city's unique heritage. This spotlight fosters community pride, as residents see their city being appreciated and celebrated by visitors. It reinforces the local identity and encourages residents to actively engage in preserving and promoting their cultural heritage. This sense of pride can have a positive ripple effect on the overall well-being and cohesion of the community.

In summary, tourism and the economic impact related to local history play a crucial role in a small American city's development. They contribute to economic growth, job creation, diversification of the local economy, preservation of historical sites, community development, promotion of local businesses, and enhanced community pride. By leveraging their historical assets, small cities can attract tourists, stimulate economic activity, and create a sustainable future for their communities.

Why is Community Engagement spurred by the history of the place important to a small American city?

Community engagement spurred by the history of a place is important to a small American city for several reasons:

Sense of Belonging and Connection: Community engagement through the history of a place fosters a sense of belonging and connection among residents. Learning about and discussing the city's history allows individuals to understand their roots, appreciate their heritage, and feel a deeper connection to their community. This shared historical knowledge can create a stronger bond among residents, leading to a more cohesive and supportive community.

Preservation and Conservation: Community engagement in the history of a place encourages residents to actively participate in the preservation and conservation of historical sites, landmarks, and cultural assets. When people are aware of the significance and value of their city's history, they are more likely to take pride in their community and work towards protecting its historical resources for future generations. Community engagement can involve volunteering, participating in restoration projects, or advocating for the preservation of local heritage.

Civic Participation and Decision-Making: Engaging with the history of a place can inspire residents to become more actively involved in civic participation and decision-making processes. By understanding the historical context of their city, residents gain insights into how it has evolved and the challenges it has faced. This knowledge empowers them to contribute their perspectives, ideas, and voices to shaping the future of their community. Community engagement in local history can include attending public meetings, joining historical societies, or participating in community planning initiatives.

Educational Opportunities: The history of a place offers rich educational opportunities for residents, especially students. Engaging with local history provides a hands-on and immersive learning experience, allowing individuals to explore and understand their city's past in a meaningful way. By incorporating local history into educational curricula and organizing educational programs, a small American city can promote lifelong learning, critical thinking, and a deeper understanding of its cultural heritage.

Cultural Celebration and Festivals: Community engagement through the history of a place often involves cultural celebrations and festivals that showcase the city's traditions, customs, and historical events. These events provide opportunities for residents to come together, celebrate their shared heritage, and showcase their unique cultural expressions. Cultural festivals and celebrations contribute to community vibrancy, attract visitors, and create a sense of pride and unity among residents.

Tourism and Economic Impact: Community engagement in the history of a place can also have economic benefits for a small American city. When residents actively participate in preserving and promoting their local history, it enhances the city's appeal as a tourist destination. Visitors are drawn to places with a rich historical narrative and an engaged local community. Tourism resulting from community engagement can stimulate the local economy, support small businesses, and create job opportunities in the tourism sector.

In summary, community engagement spurred by the history of a place is important to a small American city as it fosters a sense of belonging, promotes preservation and conservation, encourages civic participation, provides educational opportunities, supports cultural celebrations, and contributes to tourism and economic development. It strengthens the fabric of the community, empowers residents, and creates a shared sense of pride in the city's history and heritage.

Why is Research and Scholarship related to social, natural, business and scientific history of an area important to a small American city?

Research and scholarship related to the social, natural, business, and scientific history of an area are important to a small American city for several reasons:

Knowledge and Understanding: Research and scholarship deepen our knowledge and understanding of the history of an area. Through academic inquiry, historians, social scientists, environmentalists, and business scholars investigate various aspects of a city's history, shedding light on its past social, cultural, economic, and scientific developments. This research helps uncover hidden narratives, untold stories, and previously unknown contributions, providing a more comprehensive understanding of the city's heritage.

Historical Accuracy and Preservation: Research and scholarship ensure historical accuracy and the preservation of historical records and artifacts. By employing rigorous research methods and analysis, scholars can verify historical facts, challenge misconceptions, and correct inaccuracies in the historical narrative of a city. They also contribute to the documentation and preservation of primary sources, archives, oral histories, and material culture, securing valuable historical evidence for future generations.

Public Education and Outreach: Research and scholarship in local history provide opportunities for public education and outreach. Scholars can share their findings through publications, lectures, exhibitions, and public presentations. This dissemination of knowledge enhances public awareness and appreciation of the city's historical significance, fostering a deeper understanding and engagement with the community's heritage.

Cultural Tourism and Economic Development: Research and scholarship in local history can contribute to cultural tourism and economic development. Scholarly investigations often reveal unique stories, historical sites, or natural features that can attract tourists interested in exploring the city's heritage. Historical tours, guided walks, and cultural heritage routes can be developed based on research findings, creating opportunities for tourism businesses, accommodations, and local entrepreneurs to thrive.

Community Pride and Identity: Research and scholarship in local history can strengthen community pride and identity. When residents are aware of the rich historical legacy of their city, they develop a stronger sense of pride and connection to their community. Historical research can highlight the achievements, struggles, and resilience of past generations, instilling a sense of identity and continuity, and fostering community cohesion.

Planning and Policy Development: Research and scholarship in local history can inform urban planning, policy development, and decision-making processes. By understanding the historical context of a city's social, economic, and natural development, policymakers can make more informed decisions about preserving heritage buildings, protecting culturally significant areas, or revitalizing historical districts. This historical perspective helps ensure that future development aligns with the city's historical identity and values.

Collaboration and Partnerships: Research and scholarship in local history often involve collaborations and partnerships with community organizations, local institutions, and government entities. This cooperation fosters a sense of shared responsibility and mutual support for preserving and promoting the city's history. Collaborative research projects can also lead to the establishment of research centers, academic programs, or historical societies that serve as resources for ongoing scholarship and engagement.

In summary, research and scholarship related to the social, natural, business, and scientific history of an area are important to a small American city as they contribute to knowledge and understanding, ensure historical accuracy, support public education and outreach, promote cultural tourism and economic development, strengthen community pride and identity, inform planning and policy development, and encourage collaboration and partnerships. These scholarly endeavors enrich the city's historical narrative, benefit residents and visitors alike, and contribute to the overall well-being and sustainability of the community.

How can the Quality of Life in a community be enhanced through the presentation of local historical information be important to a small American city?

The presentation of local historical information can enhance the quality of life in a community in a small American city in several ways:

Cultural Enrichment: Presenting local historical information provides residents with a deeper understanding and appreciation of their community's heritage and cultural identity. It allows them to connect with their roots, traditions, and historical events that have shaped the city. This cultural enrichment enhances the quality of life by fostering a sense of pride, belonging, and shared history among residents.

Education and Learning: The presentation of local historical information offers educational opportunities for residents of all ages. It provides a platform for learning about the city's history, its evolution over time, and the people who have contributed to its development. This knowledge promotes lifelong learning, critical thinking, and a broader understanding of the world, enhancing the intellectual and personal growth of individuals within the community.

Community Engagement and Social Cohesion: Presenting local historical information encourages community engagement and social cohesion. Historical events, exhibitions, and cultural programs can bring residents together, fostering connections and relationships. Shared experiences and discussions about the city's history can build a sense of camaraderie and unity among community members, strengthening social bonds and overall community well-being.

Sense of Place and Identity: The presentation of local historical information helps residents develop a stronger sense of place and identity. It highlights the unique characteristics, landmarks, and stories that define the city. When residents have a clear understanding of their city's history, they can develop a stronger connection to their surroundings, feel a greater sense of pride, and actively contribute to the preservation and enhancement of their community.

Preservation of Historical Resources: Presenting local historical information raises awareness about the value of preserving historical resources within the community. It highlights the importance of protecting historical sites, buildings, artifacts, and documents that hold significance to the city's history. This preservation effort not only safeguards the city's heritage but also contributes to its aesthetic appeal, attracting visitors and enhancing the overall quality of life for residents.

Economic Development and Tourism: Presenting local historical information can have economic benefits for the community. Historical tourism attracts visitors who are interested in exploring the city's heritage, contributing to the local economy. The revenue generated from tourism can support local businesses, create job opportunities, and stimulate economic growth. This economic development, in turn, improves the overall quality of life for residents through increased amenities, services, and opportunities.

Sense of Continuity and Legacy: Presenting local historical information creates a sense of continuity and legacy within the community. It allows residents to recognize the contributions and achievements of previous generations and provides inspiration for future endeavors. Understanding the city's history gives residents a broader perspective of their place in the community's ongoing story, instilling a sense of purpose and responsibility for shaping its future.

In summary, the presentation of local historical information enhances the quality of life in a small American city by providing cultural enrichment, educational opportunities, promoting community engagement and social cohesion, strengthening the sense of place and identity, preserving historical resources, supporting economic development, and fostering a sense of continuity and legacy. These benefits contribute to the overall well-being, pride, and satisfaction of residents, creating a vibrant and thriving community.

How can local history be used to promote Civic Engagement in a small American city?

Local history can be effectively used to promote civic engagement in a small American city through the following approaches:

Community Dialogues and Discussions: Organize community dialogues and discussions centered around local history. These forums provide opportunities for residents to share their perspectives, memories, and stories related to the city's history. Engage community members in conversations about how historical events and figures have shaped the city and its values. Such dialogues encourage active civic participation, as residents can voice their opinions, contribute ideas, and collaborate on preserving and promoting the community's heritage.

Historical Tours and Walks: Conduct guided historical tours and walks that showcase significant sites, landmarks, and neighborhoods within the city. These tours can be led by knowledgeable guides or local historians who can provide insights into the historical significance of each location. Encouraging residents to participate in these tours fosters a sense of pride, belonging, and connection to their community. It also serves as a platform for conversations about the city's history and encourages residents to become more engaged in preserving and sharing their heritage.

Civic Education Programs: Develop civic education programs that incorporate local history into the curriculum. Introduce students to the city's historical events, civic leaders, and community organizations that have played a role in shaping the community. By understanding their city's history, students can develop a sense of civic responsibility and become active participants in community development. Engage local historians, experts, and community leaders to deliver guest lectures and workshops to deepen students' understanding of local history and its relevance to civic engagement.

Volunteer Opportunities in Historic Preservation: Provide volunteer opportunities in historic preservation initiatives. Engage residents in hands-on activities such as restoration projects, archival work, or organizing exhibitions and events related to local history. By participating in these activities, residents can directly contribute to the preservation and promotion of their community's heritage. This involvement fosters a sense of ownership, pride, and civic engagement, as residents work together to safeguard and share their history.

Collaborative Projects with Local Organizations: Foster partnerships with local organizations, such as historical societies, community centers, and cultural institutions, to develop collaborative projects that leverage local history for civic engagement. For example, organize public lectures, panel discussions, or workshops that explore the connections between local history and contemporary issues or challenges facing the community. Encourage residents to actively participate in these events, share their experiences, and collaborate on finding solutions to present-day issues.

Online Platforms and Digital Archives: Utilize online platforms and digital archives to make local historical information easily accessible to residents. Create interactive websites or social media pages that provide engaging content related to the city's history. Encourage residents to share their own historical stories, photographs, or artifacts through these platforms. By fostering an online community centered around local history, residents can connect, exchange knowledge, and contribute to the collective understanding and preservation of their community's heritage.

In summary, local history can be used as a powerful tool to promote civic engagement in a small American city. By creating spaces for dialogue, organizing historical tours, incorporating local history into education, providing volunteer opportunities, fostering collaborations, and utilizing online platforms, residents can actively participate in preserving and promoting their community's heritage. Through these initiatives, residents develop a stronger sense of civic responsibility, contribute to community development, and strengthen the overall fabric of the city.

Farmington Community Library Grants Collection

It should be kept in mind that even if you retain a Grant Writer, or, solicit more than one, by investigating possible funding opportunities yourself you will encounter items you can ask your grant writer to pursue or you can approach the funders yourself.

"The Grants Collection at the Farmington Community Library, FCL Farmington Hills location, provides the resources and guides nonprofits' need for philanthropic success. The Collection includes titles on how to start a nonprofit, manage a nonprofit, nonprofit law, nonprofit leadership, volunteers, board governance, strategic planning, prospect research, major gifts campaigns, marketing, fundraising, proposal writing, and more!

To locate titles in the Grants Collection, visit our Library Catalog.

As a member of Candid.org nationwide network of libraries, community foundations, and other nonprofit agencies, the Farmington Community Library provides visitors with free public access to Candid's products, services, and in-person classes and resources.

At FCL Farmington and Farmington Hills locations, you can access:

Foundation Directory Professional

Grants to Individuals

Foundation Maps

Additional resources and assistance to strengthen your nonprofit organization

Representatives of nonprofit and grassroots organizations and other patrons are welcome to use the databases at the Farmington Community Library at any time during our open hours."

https://www.farmlib.org/collections/grants-and-nonprofits/

The Farmington Community Library (FCL) of Farmington Hills is located at : 32737 W 12 Mile Road, Farmington Hills, Michigan

If you have a library near you that has a Grants Collection – I strongly urge you to visit it!

Potential Partnerships or Projects

Local history museums can enter into a variety of partnerships and projects to enhance their offerings, engage the community, and promote the preservation and appreciation of local history. Here are some potential partnerships and projects for local history museums:

Educational Institutions: Collaborate with schools, colleges, and universities to develop educational programs, workshops, and field trips that align with the curriculum. These partnerships can help students learn about local history in a hands-on and immersive way.

Community Organizations: Partner with local community groups, historical societies, and cultural organizations to co-host events, exhibitions, and lectures. These partnerships can foster a sense of community and provide diverse perspectives on local history.

Art and Cultural Centers: Collaborate with art galleries, performing arts centers, and cultural hubs to create interdisciplinary exhibitions or events that blend history with various forms of art and creativity.

Tourism Agencies: Work with tourism boards and agencies to promote the museum as a tourist destination and develop heritage tourism initiatives. This can bring more visitors to the museum and contribute to the local economy.

Local Businesses: Partner with local businesses for sponsorship opportunities, fundraising events, or co-promotion. Businesses could provide financial support or in-kind donations to help the museum achieve its goals.

Archives and Libraries: Partner with local archives, libraries, and historical repositories to share resources, materials, and expertise. Collaborations can lead to better research opportunities and the creation of comprehensive historical narratives.

Historic Sites: Collaborate with nearby historic sites and landmarks to create joint ticketing options, thematic tours, and combined programming that showcases the interconnectedness of local history.

Digital Initiatives: Partner with technology companies, app developers, and digital platforms to create interactive and virtual exhibits, expanding the reach of the museum beyond its physical location.

Youth and Senior Centers: Engage with youth and senior centers to develop programs that cater to different age groups, fostering intergenerational learning and cultural exchange.

Local Government: Work with local government bodies to secure funding, grants, and support for museum initiatives. Collaborate on projects that align with the municipality's cultural and historical goals.

Historical Reenactment Groups: Collaborate with historical reenactment societies to bring historical events and figures to life through interactive demonstrations and living history events.

Local Artists: Partner with local artists to create site-specific installations or exhibitions that offer artistic interpretations of local history.

Tour Operators: Collaborate with tour operators to include the museum in their guided tours and itineraries, attracting visitors who are interested in exploring the history of the area.

Nonprofit Organizations: Partner with nonprofits focused on history, culture, education, or social issues to develop joint programming that addresses shared goals and interests.

Media Outlets: Collaborate with local newspapers, radio stations, and online platforms to promote museum events, exhibitions, and educational programs, increasing visibility within the community.

By fostering these partnerships and engaging in collaborative projects, local history museums can enrich their offerings, reach new audiences, and play a more integral role in their communities' cultural and educational landscapes.

Working with the Collection

A local history museum can employ various strategies to attract interest and extract value from its collection. By creatively showcasing its artifacts, documents, and stories, the museum can engage visitors, researchers, and the community at large. Here are some ways to achieve this:

Curate Engaging Exhibitions: Develop well-designed and thematic exhibitions that highlight specific aspects of local history. Incorporate interactive displays, multimedia elements, and storytelling techniques to make the exhibits engaging and informative.

Rotate Displays: Regularly update exhibitions to keep content fresh and encourage repeat visits. This also allows the museum to showcase different parts of its collection and cater to diverse interests.

Digital Presentations: Create digital presentations or virtual tours that allow online visitors to explore the collection remotely. Virtual exhibitions and online galleries can reach a wider audience beyond the museum's physical location.

Educational Programs: Offer workshops, lectures, and educational programs that use the collection to teach various aspects of local history. These programs can cater to students, adults, families, and researchers.

Collaborative Events: Collaborate with local artists, historians, authors, and experts to co-host events like book readings, panel discussions, or workshops that revolve around the museum's collection.

Living History Events: Organize reenactments or living history events that bring historical periods to life, allowing visitors to interact with costumed interpreters and experience history firsthand.

Themed Tours: Design guided tours that delve into specific topics, time periods, or stories related to the collection. These tours can cater to different audiences and offer in-depth insights.

Artifact Workshops: Host workshops where visitors can learn about artifact conservation, preservation techniques, and the history behind specific objects in the collection.

Artifact Spotlights: Regularly feature specific artifacts on the museum's website, social media, or newsletters. Provide detailed stories, historical context, and images to create connections between the artifacts and the audience.

Collaboration with Schools: Develop educational materials and programs that align with school curricula. Invite schools for field trips, and offer guided tours that complement classroom learning.

Community Engagement: Organize events that invite the community to share their own stories, memories, and artifacts. Community-contributed content can enrich the collection and foster a sense of ownership.

Research Access: Make the collection accessible to researchers, historians, and academics. Provide facilities and resources for scholarly research, potentially leading to collaborations on publications and projects.

Digitization Efforts: Digitize parts of the collection to create an online database. This enhances accessibility for researchers and the public, and it can also lead to partnerships with digital platforms.

Collaborative Projects: Partner with other cultural institutions, universities, or historical societies on joint projects that utilize the collection for exhibitions, publications, or community initiatives.

Membership Programs: Develop membership programs that offer special access to the collection, behind-the-scenes tours, and exclusive events to encourage ongoing support and engagement.

Artisan Workshops: Host workshops that showcase traditional crafts, skills, and trades from the local history. This provides a hands-on experience and connects visitors to historical practices.

By employing these strategies, a local history museum can effectively showcase its collection, attract diverse audiences, and derive value from its artifacts in ways that are both educational and entertaining.

Raising Visibility

Raising the visibility of a local history museum in the community and surrounding areas requires a strategic approach that involves both traditional and modern marketing techniques. Here are some tips to help you effectively increase the museum's visibility:

Develop a Strong Online Presence:

Create a professional and user-friendly website that provides information about the museum, its exhibits, events, and programs.

Utilize social media platforms (Facebook, Instagram, Twitter, etc.) to share engaging content, behind-the-scenes glimpses, and upcoming events.

Regularly update the museum's blog with informative articles related to local history and the museum's collection.

Engage with the Community:

Participate in local community events, fairs, and festivals to set up informational booths or activities that showcase the museum's offerings.

Collaborate with local schools, community centers, and libraries to host educational workshops, lectures, or activities that promote the museum.

Host Special Events and Exhibitions:

Organize special events, such as opening receptions for new exhibitions, themed parties, or historical reenactments, to attract a diverse audience.

Plan exhibitions that align with current community interests or important historical anniversaries to attract more visitors.

Utilize Local Media:

Build relationships with local newspapers, magazines, radio stations, and TV stations. Send press releases about upcoming events and exhibitions.

Consider offering interviews or guest appearances on local media to discuss the museum's significance and its role in preserving local history.

Collaborate with Partners:

Partner with local businesses, tourism boards, historical societies, schools, and cultural organizations to cross-promote each other's activities and events.

Collaborate on joint projects or initiatives that highlight the shared history of the community.

Implement Word-of-Mouth Marketing:

Encourage visitors to share their experiences on social media and leave reviews on platforms like Google Maps, TripAdvisor, and Yelp.

Create a referral program that rewards visitors for bringing friends and family to the museum.

Offer Membership and Loyalty Programs:

Develop membership programs that offer exclusive benefits, such as discounts on admission, access to special events, and behind-the-scenes tours.

Reward repeat visitors with loyalty programs that offer incentives for multiple visits.

Enhance Signage and Visibility on Site:

Ensure that the museum's exterior signage is clear, visible, and attractive to passersby. Include opening hours and contact information.

Use well-designed banners, posters, and displays to promote upcoming events and exhibitions.

Engage with Schools and Educators:

Develop educational programs that align with school curricula and offer field trips to the museum. Engage teachers and educators in the process.

Provide resources for educators, such as lesson plans and activity guides, to integrate the museum's content into their teaching.

Utilize Online Advertising:

Use targeted online advertising, such as Google Ads and social media ads, to reach audiences in your community and surrounding areas.

Geo-target ads to specific regions and demographics that are likely to be interested in local history and cultural attractions.

Collect and Showcase Visitor Testimonials:

Display positive visitor testimonials and reviews prominently on your website and in your marketing materials to build credibility and trust.

Utilize Influencer Marketing:

Partner with local influencers, bloggers, and social media personalities who have a following in your community. Invite them for exclusive tours or events in exchange for coverage.

Offer Free or Discounted Admission Days:

Host occasional free or discounted admission days to encourage people who might not have visited otherwise to experience the museum.

Engage in Community Outreach:

Offer talks, workshops, or presentations about local history to community groups, schools, and clubs. This establishes the museum as a knowledgeable resource.

Stay Current and Relevant:

Keep up with current trends in museum curation, technology, and storytelling to ensure that your exhibits and programs resonate with modern audiences.

By implementing these strategies, your local history museum can increase its visibility, attract more visitors, and become a valued and integral part of the community and surrounding areas.

Volunteerism

Engaging volunteers and encouraging their participation is crucial for the success of a local history museum. Volunteers bring enthusiasm, diverse skills, and a passion for community engagement. Here are some strategies to effectively engage volunteers at your museum:

Clear Communication and Expectations:

Clearly communicate the museum's mission, goals, and the roles that volunteers will play.

Provide a detailed volunteer handbook or orientation that outlines expectations, responsibilities, and any necessary training.

Variety of Roles:

Offer a range of volunteer opportunities to accommodate various interests, skills, and time commitments. This could include roles like tour guides, event organizers, researchers, exhibit interpreters, and more.

Flexible Scheduling:

Recognize that volunteers have different availability. Offer flexible scheduling options to accommodate students, working professionals, retirees, and others.

Meaningful Tasks:

Assign tasks that are meaningful and directly contribute to the museum's mission. Volunteers are more likely to stay engaged if they see the impact of their work.

Recognition and Appreciation:

Regularly express gratitude for volunteers' efforts through thank-you notes, awards, appreciation events, and public recognition.

Highlight volunteer accomplishments in newsletters, on social media, and during museum events.

Training and Skill Development:

Provide training sessions that equip volunteers with the knowledge and skills they need to excel in their roles.

Offer opportunities for skill development and learning, such as workshops on historical research, exhibit design, or public speaking.

Collaborative Decision-Making:

Involve volunteers in decision-making processes when appropriate. Their input can lead to innovative ideas and a sense of ownership.

Feedback Mechanism:

Establish an open line of communication where volunteers can provide feedback, share their experiences, and suggest improvements.

Social and Networking Opportunities:

Organize social events, volunteer appreciation gatherings, and networking opportunities to foster a sense of community among volunteers.

Mentoring and Support:

Pair new volunteers with experienced ones to provide guidance and support. This helps newcomers feel comfortable and valued.

Celebrate Milestones:

Recognize volunteers' milestones, such as the number of hours served or years of service, with special tokens of appreciation.

Engage with Their Passions:

Learn about volunteers' interests and passions, and find ways to integrate these into their roles. This can create a more personally fulfilling experience.

Regular Updates:

Keep volunteers informed about the museum's activities, events, and achievements through regular newsletters or email updates.

Showcase Volunteer Impact:

Share stories and case studies that highlight the impact volunteers have made on the museum and the community.

Volunteer Empowerment:

Empower volunteers to take ownership of certain projects or initiatives. This can enhance their sense of responsibility and commitment.

Keep in mind that volunteers are dedicating their time and skills to support your museum's mission. Providing them with a positive and fulfilling experience will not only benefit your institution but also contribute to their personal growth and connection to the local community.

Non-Profit and Corporate Support

Generating nonprofit and corporate support for a local history museum involves building strong relationships, demonstrating the museum's value, and offering mutually beneficial opportunities. Here's how you can attract financial and in-kind support from nonprofit organizations and corporations:

For Nonprofit Support:

Research and Identify Potential Partners:

Identify local foundations, trusts, and nonprofit organizations that align with the museum's mission and goals.

Craft Compelling Proposals:

Create detailed proposals that highlight the museum's impact on education, community engagement, cultural preservation, and the broader community.

Personalize Communication:

Tailor your communication to each potential donor's interests and priorities. Show how their support will directly contribute to the causes they care about.

Highlight Collaboration Opportunities:

Emphasize the potential for collaborative projects, joint events, and shared resources that align with the nonprofit's mission.

Showcase Impact and Outcomes:

Use success stories, case studies, and statistics to demonstrate the positive impact the museum has on the community and how nonprofit support can amplify that impact.

Offer Recognition and Benefits:

Provide recognition and benefits, such as logo placement, exclusive events, and special access, to acknowledge the nonprofit's support.

Cultivate Relationships:

Build and maintain relationships with nonprofit leaders and representatives through meetings, networking events, and regular updates.

For Corporate Support:

Identify Relevant Corporations:

Identify corporations with a history of philanthropic giving, a commitment to community engagement, or a connection to the museum's mission.

Demonstrate Alignment:

Show how the museum's goals align with the corporate social responsibility initiatives and values of potential corporate partners.

Create Customized Sponsorship Packages:

Develop sponsorship packages that offer various levels of support and corresponding benefits, such as logo placement, brand exposure, and employee engagement opportunities.

Pitch Employee Engagement Opportunities:

Highlight opportunities for employees to volunteer at the museum, participate in team-building events, or engage in educational programs.

Provide Data on Audience Reach:

Share information on the museum's visitor demographics, online presence, and event attendance to showcase the exposure corporate partners can receive.

Leverage In-Kind Support:

Request in-kind support from corporations, such as donations of goods, services, or technology that the museum can use to enhance its operations.

Offer Exclusive Events:

Provide corporate sponsors with exclusive access to museum events, private tours, and other unique experiences as a way of expressing appreciation.

Highlight Long-Term Impact:

Explain how corporate support can contribute to the long-term sustainability of the museum, enriching the community for years to come.

Personalize Engagement:

Build personal relationships with corporate decision-makers and representatives through networking, meetings, and appreciation events.

Showcase Success Stories:

Share stories of successful partnerships with other corporations to demonstrate the benefits of supporting the museum.

Provide Recognition and Publicity:

Offer prominent recognition through museum signage, press releases, social media, and other promotional channels.

Remember that building and maintaining strong relationships with both nonprofit organizations and corporations is key to generating sustainable support. Tailor your approach to each potential partner, focusing on their specific interests and how their support can contribute to the museum's growth and impact.

Alternatives for the Future

Immediate Actions

In Louisiana there was a history museum in a very old town. It was in an out of the way location and did not get many visitors. It burned to the ground. So – the State offered to rebuild it and they did but they paired it up with the local welcome center for the area. This suited the situation, however, no one visited other than the visitors popping in to the welcome center. So the director of the museum started to have a farmer's market. He rented out table space and left a donation box outside during the time it was taking place. They then had income from the market as well as donations.

For many communities this would solve two problems – the lack of fresh produce and provide a potential source of income for the museum. From spring to late autumn it could take place. The way to get started is just to roll it out and see what happens. You could set up a tent or have someone run it for you.

The materials that you have are chock full of information and materials that can be offered for sale and reuse. Many of the photos can be offered separately, bundled into groups for uses as cards, in books, to accompany magazine articles and a whole host of other things.

The varied ethnic background of the makeup of the people who have lived and worked here is a bonanza. The people who are living and working, now, whether they just arrived yesterday or lived here their whole lives are probably not aware that people just like them came here to this wonderful city in America and made a life for themselves. Some of them gained fortunes. Some gained fame. Most lived safe lives in a caring community with interesting things to do and nice people to talk with.

We spoke about financing and grants and things but specific items would be – if you settled on replacing the drop ceiling instead of repairing or showing off whatever is above it – then you can reach out to the makers of the materials or the distributors. These are major corporations and they do offer discounts and sometimes financial assistance or will make entire donations dependent upon what is happening. This goes for the carpeting, the painting, and, though its kind of late for that now, things like the HVAC systems. Reaching out, of course, doesn't mean anyone will reach back but in this case the contacts are important and will be necessary as this goes forward.

Patents
Intellectual Property

How to buy expired patents

updated May 11, 2023 · 2min read

A patent is a license that allows an inventor to be the only person or company allowed to make, use, or sell a specific invention. The patent is granted by the United States Patent and Trademark Office (USPTO) after the submission of an application and drawings. If that invention is not already patented, the inventor receives a patent after the materials are reviewed. Patents do not last forever, though, and they can lapse, providing the opportunity for someone else possibly to purchase the expired patent.

Utility patents expire four, eight, and 12 years after issuance of the patent if the maintenance fees are not paid at these points in time. The patent actually expires at 3.5 years, 7.5 years, and 11.5 years, but there is a six-month grace period in which to pay the maintenance fee. Once the fee is paid, the patent is renewed.

It is possible for the patent owner to reinstate the patent, if it expires, by paying a surcharge in addition to the maintenance fee. It's also possible for the patent holder to put the expired patent up for sale and sell the patent and their rights to someone else who could renew the expired patent by paying the fees. It is not possible for someone else to refile for an expired patent—that application would be denied, since there is an existing invention recognized by the USPTO.

If the maintenance fees are paid, a utility patent lasts for a total of 20 years. The patent expiration date for design and plant patents is 14 years after issuance.

Expired patents and public domain

After a patent has been in place for 20 years for utility patents and 14 years for design and plant patents, the invention becomes part of the public domain. This means the invention no longer has patent protection and is no longer off limits, so anyone can make, use, or sell the invention without infringement.

Where to find expired patents

If you are wondering how to find expired patents, follow these steps:

Do a patent search through the USPTO.

Select USPTO Patent Full-Text and Image Database (PatFT).

Select Advanced Search.

Input a date range or a specific date and begin the search.

Choose the patent you want to research.

Copy the patent number.

Go to Public Patent Application Information Retrieval.

Indicate that you are not a robot.

Search using the patent number.

Check to see if the patent is active, expired, or abandoned.

If it is expired, you can proceed with trying to buy it.

How to buy an expired patent

Once you've located a patent that has expired, you can contact the patent owner and negotiate a sale. You can buy the invention and all rights to it, including the patent. You then renew the patent by paying the lapsed fees.

If the patent is past the 20- or 14-year mark (depending on the type of patent), you cannot renew the patent, but you can still own the product and any other materials and information you purchase from the inventor.

Managing and protecting your intellectual property—whether it is your own that you create, or someone else's intellectual property that you purchase—is important. You may want to work with an online services provider to help ensure that your intellectual property is adequately protected.

Learn More by contacting Brette Sember, J.D.

Brette Sember, J.D., practiced law in New York, including divorce, mediation, family law, adoption,

Here are 30 fundraising ideas for a small city history museum:

Membership Drive: Promote annual museum memberships with special benefits.

Silent Auction: Organize a silent auction featuring donated items or experiences.

History Trivia Night: Host a fun trivia night with history-related questions.

Museum Store Sale: Offer discounts or special promotions at the museum store.

Corporate Sponsorships: Seek out local businesses to sponsor museum events or exhibits.

Historical Costume Party: Organize a themed costume party with a historical twist.

Community Yard Sale: Encourage the community to donate items for a fundraising yard sale.

Crowdfunding Campaign: Create an online campaign to raise funds from supporters worldwide.

Corporate Volunteer Days: Invite local businesses to volunteer at the museum and donate funds.

Storytelling Events: Host storytelling sessions where community members share their historical experiences.

Craft Workshops: Offer craft workshops inspired by historical techniques or artifacts.

Movie Night: Organize a screening of a classic or historically relevant film.

Car Wash: Gather volunteers to host a car wash fundraiser in a visible location.

Guest Lectures: Invite guest speakers to give lectures on historical topics.

Community Cookbook: Create a cookbook featuring historical recipes and sell it as a fundraiser.

Walking Tours: Organize guided historical walking tours of the city, charging a fee for participation.

Partner with Local Schools: Collaborate with schools to organize fundraising events or competitions.

Photo Contest: Hold a photography contest centered around the city's historical landmarks.

Donation Boxes: Place donation boxes at local businesses or in high-traffic areas.

Gala or Benefit Dinner: Host a formal fundraising event with guest speakers and entertainment.

Historical Reenactments: Stage historical reenactments or living history events to engage the community.

Corporate Matching Programs: Encourage employees of local companies to participate in matching gift programs.

Online Auction: Organize an online auction platform to sell unique historical items or experiences.

Art Exhibition: Hold an art exhibition featuring local artists inspired by the city's history.

Scavenger Hunt: Create a city-wide scavenger hunt with historical clues and charge a participation fee.

Grant Applications: Research and apply for grants available to support historical preservation and education.

Pop-Up Museum: Collaborate with local businesses to create temporary historical exhibits in their spaces.

Historical Calendar: Design and sell a historical calendar featuring photographs and important dates.

Donation Drives: Collect specific items or artifacts through targeted donation drives.

Sponsor a Brick: Allow individuals or businesses to sponsor bricks or tiles engraved with their names in a prominent museum area.

Remember to tailor these ideas to suit the specific needs and resources of your small city history museum. Good luck with your fundraising efforts!

Here are the names of 100 organizations that provide grants to small history museums. Please note that grant availability may vary, and it's important to research each organization for specific eligibility criteria and application details:

National Endowment for the Humanities (NEH)

Institute of Museum and Library Services (IMLS)

American Association for State and Local History (AASLH)

National Trust for Historic Preservation

The Andrew W. Mellon Foundation

American Alliance of Museums (AAM)

The Getty Foundation

The Kress Foundation

The Hearst Foundations

The Richard H. Driehaus Foundation

The Samuel H. Kress Foundation

The Henry Luce Foundation

The Gladys Krieble Delmas Foundation

The Charles Lafitte Foundation

The J.M. Kaplan Fund

The Graham Foundation

The Graham Foundation for Advanced Studies in the Fine Arts

The Lawrence Foundation

The David and Lucile Packard Foundation

The Ford Foundation

The John D. and Catherine T. MacArthur Foundation

The Robert W. Woodruff Foundation

The M.J. Murdock Charitable Trust

The John Templeton Foundation

The Community Foundation for Greater Atlanta

The Citi Foundation

The Barr Foundation

The Hewlett Foundation

The Charles Stewart Mott Foundation

The W.K. Kellogg Foundation

The William and Flora Hewlett Foundation

The John S. and James L. Knight Foundation

The Walton Family Foundation

The Doris Duke Charitable Foundation

The Laura and John Arnold Foundation

The Alfred P. Sloan Foundation

The Duke Endowment

The Winthrop Rockefeller Foundation

The Jessie Ball duPont Fund

The Lilly Endowment

The Arthur Vining Davis Foundations

The Mott Foundation

The Simons Foundation

The Houston Endowment

The George Gund Foundation

The Robert R. McCormick Foundation

The Richard King Mellon Foundation

The Annenberg Foundation

The W.M. Keck Foundation

The William Penn Foundation

The Kellogg Foundation

The Spencer Foundation

The Andy Warhol Foundation for the Visual Arts

The Ewing Marion Kauffman Foundation

The Lynde and Harry Bradley Foundation

The George Lucas Educational Foundation

The Windgate Foundation

The William T. Grant Foundation

The McKnight Foundation

The Pritzker Traubert Foundation

The Surdna Foundation

The Geraldine R. Dodge Foundation

The Alfred P. Sloan Foundation

The Teagle Foundation

The Helmsley Charitable Trust

The William Randolph Hearst Foundation

The Gordon and Betty Moore Foundation

The Alfred P. Sloan Foundation

The Andrew W. Mellon Foundation

The Walter and Elise Haas Fund

The Carnegie Corporation of New York

The Jessie Smith Noyes Foundation

The Theodora L. and Stanley H. Feldberg Charitable Trust

The National Endowment for the Arts (NEA)

The Graham Foundation for Advanced Studies in the Fine Arts

The Elizabeth Firestone Graham Foundation

The Greater Houston Community Foundation

The Russell Sage Foundation

The Theodor Jacobsen Observatory

The Stephen and Tabitha King Foundation

The Carl and Marilynn Thoma Foundation

The Kreielsheimer Foundation

The Samuel I. Newhouse Foundation

The Daniel and Florence Guggenheim Foundation

The Peter Jay Sharp Foundation

The John Simon Guggenheim Memorial Foundation

The Laura and John Arnold Foundation

The Teagle Foundation

The Robert Rauschenberg Foundation

The National Science Foundation (NSF)

The Arizona Humanities Council

The California Humanities

The Florida Humanities Council

The Illinois Humanities Council

The Indiana Humanities Council

The Kansas Humanities Council

The Kentucky Humanities Council

The Massachusetts Foundation for the Humanities

The Minnesota Humanities Center

The Missouri Humanities Council

Please note that this is not an exhaustive list, and it's always a good idea to explore local and regional foundations and grant opportunities as well. Make sure to review each organization's website for the most up-to-date information on their grant programs.

Fundraising can be fun and interesting —

Having a group set up a raffle or raffles for items that people and companies donate can be very rewarding.

For example – these are some examples of what airline companies might offer :

Airlines that offer donation tickets for charity include :

Southwest Airlines: Takes donation requests online at least 60 days before an event date.

Delta: Considers sponsorship requests at least 90 days before an event, from any nonprofit that is serving communities in which it works or flies.

JetBlue: Has a simple online form for any charity near a city in which it operates (more than 90).

Airlift Hope NC-TN: Serves North Carolina and Tennessee.

Angel Flight Central: Serves Illinois, Indiana, Iowa, Kansas, Nebraska, North Dakota, Minnesota, Missouri, South Dakota, and Wisconsin.

Angel Flight Mid-Atlantic: Serves D.C., Delaware, Kentucky, Maryland, Michigan, Ohio, Pennsylvania (shared), Virginia, and West Virginia.

Here are several other ideas and approaches to begin with :

Historical Costume Gala: Host a themed gala where attendees dress up in historical costumes from different eras. Include historical entertainment, music, and interactive exhibits.

Trivia Night: Organize a history-themed trivia night where participants can test their knowledge of local and global history. Charge an entry fee and offer prizes for the winning teams.

Heritage Food Festival: Collaborate with local restaurants to showcase historical and traditional dishes from different time periods. Attendees can sample the food and learn about its significance.

Historical Scavenger Hunt: Create a city-wide scavenger hunt with historical clues and landmarks. Participants pay an entry fee to participate and have a chance to win prizes.

Time-Traveling Photography Exhibit: Curate a photography exhibit that juxtaposes historical photos with modern reenactments of the same scenes. Charge an admission fee for the exhibition.

Historical Lecture Series: Invite historians, authors, and experts to give talks on various aspects of local history. Charge a fee for entry and offer attendees the chance to learn while supporting the museum.

Artifact Auction: Host an auction featuring donated items or replicas of historical artifacts. Auction off items related to local history, and donate the proceeds to the museum.

Vintage Fashion Show: Organize a fashion show showcasing vintage clothing and accessories from different eras. Attendees can purchase tickets to watch the show and learn about historical fashion trends.

Historical Home Tour: Collaborate with homeowners to organize a historical home tour, allowing attendees to explore local historic homes and architecture for a ticket fee.

Escape Room Challenge: Create a history-themed escape room with puzzles and challenges related to local historical events. Teams pay to participate, and successful participants win prizes.

History Trivia Marathon: Host a 24-hour history trivia marathon where participants take turns answering trivia questions. Collect pledges based on the number of hours they can participate.

Interactive Historical Play: Work with local theater groups to put on an interactive play that brings historical events to life. Charge admission and encourage audience engagement.

Vintage Fair or Market: Organize a vintage fair featuring vendors selling antique items, collectibles, and vintage clothing. Charge vendors for stalls and visitors for entry.

Historical Ghost Tour: Conduct guided ghost tours that delve into the haunted history of local landmarks. Charge participants a fee to join the tour and hear spooky historical tales.

Historical Craft Workshops: Offer workshops where participants can learn historical crafts, such as candle making, quill writing, or traditional cooking. Charge a fee for participation.

Themed Movie Nights: Screen historical movies or documentaries in an outdoor or indoor setting. Charge an admission fee and provide refreshments for a cozy movie night.

Historical Gaming Tournament: Host a gaming tournament featuring historical video games or board games set in different eras. Participants pay an entry fee, and winners receive prizes.

History-inspired Art Auction: Invite local artists to create artwork inspired by historical events or figures. Auction off the artwork, with a portion of the proceeds benefiting the museum.

Time Capsule Fundraiser: Encourage community members to contribute items for a time capsule that will be buried and opened in the future. Participants pay a fee to include items in the capsule.

Vintage Photo Booth Fundraiser: Set up a vintage-themed photo booth with props and backdrops representing different historical eras. Attendees can pay for souvenir photos.

You can tailor these ideas to fit your museum's theme, resources, and audience. Make sure to promote your fundraising events through various channels, including social media, local newspapers, and community bulletin boards, to ensure a successful turnout.

Cooperation among departments in an organization is crucial for several reasons:

Enhanced Communication: Cooperation fosters open lines of communication between departments. It allows for the sharing of information, knowledge, and expertise, enabling departments to stay informed about each other's activities, goals, and challenges. This, in turn, helps avoid misunderstandings, conflicts, and duplication of efforts.

Efficient Resource Utilization: When departments cooperate, they can pool their resources, including personnel, finances, and equipment. By sharing resources, organizations can optimize their utilization and avoid unnecessary duplication. This leads to cost savings and improved efficiency in achieving organizational objectives.

Synergy and Innovation: Cooperation among departments encourages the exchange of ideas and perspectives. Different departments bring unique expertise and viewpoints to the table, which can spark creativity, innovation, and problem-solving. Collaboration across departments often leads to better solutions and new approaches to challenges.

Streamlined Workflows: Cooperation helps streamline workflows and processes. When departments work together, they can identify bottlenecks, eliminate redundant steps, and establish efficient handoffs between different stages of work. This can lead to smoother operations, improved productivity, and faster response times.

Customer Focus: Effective cooperation allows organizations to align their efforts and work towards a common goal of delivering value to customers or stakeholders. By coordinating their activities, departments can provide a seamless and positive experience for customers, ensuring their needs are met comprehensively.

Cross-Functional Learning and Development: Cooperation enables employees to learn from colleagues in different departments. This cross-functional learning expands employees' knowledge base, enhances their skills, and promotes professional growth. It also encourages a culture of continuous learning and collaboration within the organization.

Organizational Unity: Cooperation fosters a sense of unity and shared purpose among different departments. When departments collaborate effectively, they develop a collective identity and work towards common organizational objectives. This unity strengthens the overall organizational culture and creates a positive and supportive work environment.

Adaptability to Change: In today's dynamic business environment, organizations must be adaptable and responsive to change. Cooperation among departments facilitates agility and adaptability by breaking down silos and promoting information flow. It enables organizations to respond quickly to market shifts, customer demands, and emerging opportunities.

Overall, cooperation among departments is essential for organizations to function effectively and achieve their goals. It promotes efficiency, innovation, and collaboration, creating a cohesive and high-performing organization.

A natural partner for the Museum and its ongoing efforts to do the work assigned as well as ensure a future of opportunity is the local Library. Both organizations serve the community in similar ways. Information is storehoused and must be deliverable upon demand. Information is also marketed or displayed in an open way, so that, citizens can be made aware of information they will find entertaining, useful or critical in pursuing their personal goals.

The local library can be a natural and valuable partner for the work done by a local history museum due to the complementary nature of their missions and the shared goals of promoting education, preserving history, and serving the community. Here are some reasons why the local library and history museum make excellent partners:

Shared Resources: Both the library and history museum often house extensive collections of books, documents, photographs, and artifacts related to local history. By collaborating, they can pool their resources and provide more comprehensive access to historical materials.

Research Support: Libraries are experienced in research assistance, offering resources and expertise to help individuals explore historical topics. A history museum can refer visitors to the library for in-depth research needs.

Educational Programming: Both institutions prioritize educational programming. The museum can collaborate with the library to offer joint workshops, lectures, and presentations that provide a deeper understanding of local history.

Community Engagement: Libraries and history museums are hubs of community engagement. By working together, they can attract a broader audience and foster a sense of community pride and involvement.

Public Programming: Libraries often host book clubs, author talks, and public lectures. The museum can participate by contributing speakers or co-hosting events related to local history.

Exhibit Enhancements: Libraries can host exhibits or displays related to local history that complement the museum's exhibitions. This expands the reach of historical content to a broader audience.

Archival Collaboration: Both institutions may have archival collections. Collaborating on the preservation, digitization, and sharing of archival materials can maximize their impact.

Promotion and Cross-Marketing: Libraries have strong community connections and promotional channels. Joint marketing efforts can increase the visibility of both the library and the museum.

Cultural and Heritage Partnerships: Libraries and history museums contribute to the cultural heritage of a community. Working together, they can amplify the community's understanding of its past.

Educational Support: Schools often collaborate with both libraries and history museums for educational purposes. Joint initiatives can provide students with a well-rounded historical learning experience.

Local Author and Historian Engagement: Both institutions can invite local authors and historians to speak about their work. Collaborative events encourage community members to engage with local history creators.

Community Spaces: Libraries and history museums often provide meeting spaces. Collaborative workshops, lectures, and events can be hosted in these spaces.

Interactive Learning: Libraries and history museums can jointly create interactive learning experiences, combining resources and technologies to engage visitors in innovative ways.

Children's and Youth Programs: Libraries and history museums both serve children and youth. Collaborative programs can inspire a love for history and learning from a young age.

Public Funding and Advocacy: Collaborating on grant applications and advocating for local history preservation can be more effective when institutions work together.

In essence, the local library and history museum can leverage their respective strengths to create a more comprehensive and impactful experience for the community. Their partnership can promote a deeper understanding of local history, enhance educational opportunities, and enrich the cultural fabric of the community.

Opportunities for Research and Invention

Opportunities abound. With many young families in the area, many adults engaged in professional life, both blue collar and white collar, as well as seniors and other citizens of leisure the museum has a large potential following that includes just about every one of the citizens in your community.

A local history museum can offer a range of opportunities for research and invention that go beyond traditional exhibits and collections. Here are several ways in which a local history museum can inspire research and invention:

Archival Research: Museums often house extensive archives containing documents, photographs, maps, and records. Researchers can delve into these archives to uncover forgotten stories, trace family histories, and contribute to historical scholarship.

Artifact Analysis: Researchers and inventors can study artifacts to understand their historical significance, construction techniques, and cultural context. This can lead to insights about past technologies and craftsmanship.

Material Science Investigations: Researchers can analyze materials used in historical artifacts to learn about their properties, degradation, and preservation methods. This knowledge can be applied to modern conservation and material science.

Innovation from the Past: Exploring historical technologies and inventions can inspire modern innovations. Researchers can reinterpret old techniques and adapt them to contemporary challenges.

Museum-University Partnerships: Collaborations between museums and universities can foster joint research projects, allowing academics and students to engage with the museum's resources and contribute to its mission.

Digital Reconstruction: Researchers can use historical records and artifacts to digitally reconstruct lost or damaged items, buildings, or landscapes. This can provide valuable insights into the past.

Educational Curriculum Development: Researchers and educators can collaborate to develop educational materials and programs that incorporate local history into school curricula. This fosters a deeper understanding of the region's heritage.

Interactive Exhibits: Inventors and technologists can work with museums to develop interactive exhibits that engage visitors in new and innovative ways, blending history with technology.

Community Collaboration: Museums can invite community members to contribute their stories, memories, and artifacts, forming a collaborative approach to local history preservation.

Environmental and Geographic Research: Studying historical landscapes, flora, and fauna can reveal insights into past ecosystems and environmental changes, which can inform modern environmental research and conservation efforts.

Architectural Conservation and Restoration: Researchers can analyze historical architecture and collaborate with architects to restore or preserve heritage buildings using modern techniques.

Cultural Revival: Local history museums can support cultural revival efforts by preserving and revitalizing traditional practices, crafts, and languages.

Storytelling and Oral Histories: Researchers can conduct oral history interviews with community members to capture personal stories and experiences, enriching the museum's narrative.

Genealogy and Family History: Museums can offer resources for genealogical research, allowing individuals to explore their family histories and connect with their heritage.

Artistic Interpretation: Artists, writers, and creators can draw inspiration from historical narratives and artifacts to produce new works of art, literature, and multimedia content.

Futuristic Visions: Researchers and inventors can collaborate with museums to envision how historical events might have played out differently, encouraging speculative and creative thinking.

Public Health and Medicine: Researchers can study historical medical practices, health challenges, and epidemics to gain insights into the evolution of public health and medicine.

Sustainable Practices: Investigate historical practices related to agriculture, resource use, and craftsmanship to explore sustainable living solutions.

Technology and Communication: Study the evolution of communication tools, from early writing systems to printing presses, to gain insights into how technology has shaped human interaction.

Entrepreneurial Inspiration: Exploring the stories of historical entrepreneurs can inspire modern business ideas and models, while also showcasing the challenges and successes of the past.

By fostering a culture of research, innovation, and collaboration, local history museums can become hubs of creativity that contribute not only to preserving the past but also to shaping the future.

Methods of Communication to Increase Cooperation

Ask what the other departments are doing – in this case with special focus on the library. If the library is talking about Native Americans then that would be a good partnering opportunity.

Also tell the other departments what is going on. If the Museum plans on cooperating in some way with the library's focus on Native Americans then let your Economic Director know about it.

If there is going to be a focus on something the museum is doing, like about the new parts for the airplane that will be displayed, then let the library know and the Economic Director and others. The information you have may spur some response from the library. As for the business aspect of downtown that is something that can be shared locally and is also something that can be shared at tourist locations like the airport and to the state for their tourism work.

These things do not produce immediate results but they do provide new avenues to talk about your local community with others.

A local history museum can utilize a variety of communication methods to increase attendance, patronage, and engagement with local schools and community organizations. Here are some effective communication strategies:

Website: Maintain an informative and user-friendly website that provides details about exhibits, events, educational programs, and contact information. Keep the website up-to-date with current offerings.

Social Media: Use platforms like Facebook, Instagram, Twitter, and LinkedIn to share news, updates, behind-the-scenes content, and event announcements. Engage with followers by responding to comments and messages.

Email Newsletters: Send regular email newsletters to subscribers, featuring upcoming events, workshops, and special offers. Provide valuable content related to local history and community engagement.

Press Releases: Write and distribute press releases to local media outlets whenever the museum has newsworthy events, exhibitions, or collaborations. This can increase media coverage and public awareness.

Collaboration with Schools: Reach out to local schools and educational institutions to offer tailored programs, field trips, and workshops aligned with their curricula. Maintain communication with teachers and administrators.

Partnerships with Community Organizations: Collaborate with local community organizations, historical societies, libraries, and cultural groups to cross-promote events and initiatives.

Community Bulletin Boards: Post flyers and announcements about museum events on community bulletin boards in public spaces, schools, libraries, and local businesses.

Local Newspapers and Magazines: Advertise in local newspapers and magazines, and also submit articles or op-eds related to local history and museum activities.

Radio and Podcasts: Engage with local radio stations and podcasts for interviews, discussions, or sponsored segments about the museum's offerings.

Public Speaking: Offer presentations about the museum's mission and programs at community meetings, local events, and town hall gatherings.

Open Houses and Tours: Host regular open house events and guided tours to introduce the museum to new audiences and encourage repeat visits.

Educational Brochures: Create informative brochures outlining the museum's educational programs, workshops, and offerings for schools and educators.

Online Advertising: Use targeted online advertising, such as Google Ads and social media ads, to reach local audiences interested in history, education, and cultural activities.

Community Events and Festivals: Participate in local community events and festivals with a booth or exhibit, showcasing the museum's offerings and engaging with attendees.

Posters and Flyers: Design eye-catching posters and flyers to promote upcoming exhibitions, events, and programs in high-traffic areas.

Engage Local Influencers: Collaborate with local influencers, bloggers, and community leaders who can help spread the word about the museum to their followers.

Mobile Apps: Develop a mobile app that provides information about exhibits, events, guided tours, and interactive experiences for visitors.

Promote Membership Benefits: Highlight the benefits of museum membership, such as exclusive events, discounts, and special access, to encourage ongoing patronage.

Community Workshops: Organize workshops and educational sessions focused on local history topics that can attract a diverse range of participants.

Feedback and Surveys: Encourage visitors, schools, and organizations to provide feedback through surveys. Use the feedback to improve services and tailor offerings to their preferences.

Utilizing a combination of these strategies will help your local history museum effectively reach out to the community, schools, and organizations, ultimately increasing attendance and fostering engagement.

On the Matter of Products that can be offered by the Museum from presently available materials

Item 1

Here is a list of printed and digital materials created from historical images that can be offered for sale:

Printed Materials:

Photographic Prints: High-quality prints of historical images, suitable for framing and display.

Postcards: Reproductions of historical images on postcards, which can be collected or sent as souvenirs.

Calendars: Historical image calendars featuring different images for each month.

Coffee Table Books: Books that showcase a collection of historical images with accompanying narratives and descriptions.

Art Prints: Fine art prints of selected historical images, suitable for framing as decorative pieces.

Greeting Cards: Cards featuring historical images for various occasions, such as birthdays, holidays, or anniversaries.

Maps: Reproductions of historical maps, either as standalone prints or incorporated into other products, such as wall decals or puzzles.

Notepads and Stationery: Stationery sets featuring historical images, including notepads, envelopes, and writing paper.

Digital Materials:

Digital Downloads: High-resolution digital versions of historical images that customers can purchase and download for personal or commercial use.

E-books: Digital books or guides that explore the history behind a collection of historical images.

Desktop Wallpapers: Digital wallpapers featuring historical images that can be downloaded and used as computer or mobile device backgrounds.

Digital Posters: Digital versions of historical posters that can be downloaded and printed by customers in various sizes.

Slideshow Presentations: Digital presentations featuring historical images with accompanying narratives and descriptions, suitable for educational or informative purposes.

Screensavers: Digital screensavers featuring a rotating collection of historical images.

Digital Collages: Collages of historical images arranged in a visually appealing manner, available for digital download or printing.

Virtual Reality (VR) Experiences: Immersive VR experiences that allow users to explore historical locations or events through a combination of historical images, 3D reconstructions, and narratives.

Remember to consider copyright and licensing aspects when offering historical images for sale to ensure proper usage rights are obtained for commercial purposes.

Item 2

Reproductions

Here is a list of items that can be reproduced from a museum collection and offered for sale:

Reproduction Art Prints: High-quality reproductions of famous artworks or historical pieces from the museum's collection, suitable for framing and display.

Museum Catalogs: Publications that showcase the museum's collection, including detailed descriptions and images of significant artifacts and artworks.

Postcards: Reproductions of artworks, artifacts, or photographs from the museum's collection on postcards, which can be collected or sent as souvenirs.

T-shirts and Apparel: Clothing items featuring designs inspired by artworks or museum logos, such as t-shirts, hoodies, or hats.

Stationery and Notepads: Stationery sets, including notepads, envelopes, and writing paper, featuring artwork or historical images from the museum's collection.

Home Decor Items: Decorative items like throw pillows, blankets, or wall decals with designs inspired by artworks or historical motifs.

Jewelry: Jewelry pieces inspired by artifacts or motifs from the museum's collection, such as necklaces, earrings, or bracelets.

Ceramic Mugs and Drinkware: Mugs featuring artwork or historical images from the museum's collection.

Puzzles: Jigsaw puzzles featuring images of famous artworks or historical scenes from the museum's collection.

Magnets and Keychains: Small souvenirs featuring miniature reproductions of artworks or historical artifacts from the museum's collection.

Art Cards and Greeting Cards: Cards featuring reproductions of artworks or historical images, suitable for various occasions.

Replica Artifacts: Reproductions or scaled-down replicas of historical artifacts from the museum's collection, allowing visitors to own a piece of history.

Books and Publications: Books, guides, or exhibition catalogs that delve into specific aspects of the museum's collection, providing in-depth information and insights.

Digital Downloads: Digital files, such as high-resolution images or ebooks, that customers can purchase and download for personal or educational use.

Limited Edition Collectibles: Limited edition or signed collectible items, such as prints, books, or specially crafted artifacts, available in limited quantities for collectors. It is essential for the museum to consider copyright and licensing agreements when reproducing and selling items from its collection to ensure compliance and proper authorization for commercial use.

Item 3

Solicit a Teacher or Teachers to come and view the collections and then cooperate with them to create Lesson Plans.

These lesson plans can be offered for sale by the museum, in collaboration with the teacher, or, as their numbers grow, all collected together into a book or set of materials that can be sold, leased or given away.

Item 4

Learn how to write grants and solicit funds :

Example from edX -   Grant Writing and Crowdfunding for Public Libraries

(Adapt for Museums)

Example form edX -   Professional Communication: Business Writing and Storytelling

Example from coursera -   Fundraising and Development

Item 5

Support Materials to Gain Public Attention and Prepare for Fundraising

Creating compelling support materials is essential for gaining public attention and preparing for successful fundraising efforts for a local history museum. These materials should effectively convey the museum's mission, goals, and the impact of its work. Here are some key support materials to consider:

Mission Statement and Vision: Clearly articulate the museum's mission and vision statements. These should succinctly explain the purpose and values of the museum.

Brochures and Pamphlets: Design visually appealing brochures that provide an overview of the museum's history, exhibits, programs, and upcoming events. Include high-quality images and engaging text.

Annual Reports: Develop annual reports that highlight the museum's achievements, financial information, community impact, and future goals. Use infographics and stories to make the report engaging.

Case for Support Document: Create a comprehensive document that outlines the museum's goals, needs, and the reasons why supporters should contribute. Include success stories and statistics to make a compelling case.

Donor Recognition Levels: Design a donor recognition chart that outlines the different giving levels and the benefits associated with each level of support. This helps potential donors understand the value of their contributions.

Fact Sheets: Develop fact sheets about specific exhibitions, programs, or projects that the museum is fundraising for. Include details about the historical significance and impact of these initiatives.

Project Descriptions: Write detailed project descriptions for specific fundraising initiatives. Explain the goals, timeline, budget, and intended outcomes of each project.

Testimonials and Stories: Gather testimonials from visitors, volunteers, and community members who have benefited from the museum. Share personal stories that highlight the museum's impact.

Historical Impact Statement: Craft a statement that illustrates the museum's role in preserving and promoting local history. Explain how the museum contributes to the cultural heritage of the community.

Educational Materials: Develop educational materials that schools and educators can use. This could include lesson plans, activity guides, and resource lists that align with the curriculum.

Interactive Maps or Timelines: Create interactive maps or timelines that showcase the historical significance of the local area. Use visuals to highlight key events and landmarks.

Virtual Tour or Video: Produce a virtual tour video that takes viewers through the museum's exhibits and highlights. This can give potential donors a sense of what to expect.

Impact Infographics: Design visually appealing infographics that showcase the museum's impact, such as the number of visitors, educational programs, and community partnerships.

Collaboration Partners: List local schools, community organizations, and businesses that the museum collaborates with. This demonstrates community engagement and partnerships.

Financial Transparency: Share financial information that highlights the museum's financial health, responsible stewardship of funds, and the impact of donations.

Interactive Website: Create an engaging website that houses all the support materials, making them easily accessible to potential donors and the public.

Press Kit: Assemble a press kit with high-resolution images, press releases, and background information about the museum. This helps media outlets cover your fundraising efforts.

Donation Form or Online Portal: Develop user-friendly donation forms or an online portal where supporters can easily contribute to the museum's fundraising campaigns.

Social Media Content: Craft engaging posts for social media platforms that highlight the museum's impact, success stories, and upcoming fundraising events.

Community Impact Reports: Publish reports that detail how the museum's work has positively impacted the local community, including educational outcomes, cultural enrichment, and tourism.

Creating a strong set of support materials helps establish the credibility and importance of your local history museum's work. These materials should resonate with potential supporters and inspire them to contribute to the museum's fundraising initiatives.

Printed in Great Britain
by Amazon